COMMITTED
TO QUAKERISM

A CHRISTIAN COMMUNITY

SYLVIA AND BARRY
SUTCLIFFE

6245

RMEP

RELIGIOUS AND MORAL EDUCATION PRESS

Religious and Moral Education Press
An imprint of Chansitor Publications Ltd,
a wholly owned subsidary of Hymns Ancient & Modern Ltd
St Mary's Works, St Mary's Plain
Norwich, Norfolk NR3 3BH

First published 1995

ISBN 1-85175-028-2

Acknowledgements
The Authors and Publisher would like to thank the
members and attenders of the Jesus Lane Meeting, Cambridge,
particularly those whose interviews appear in this book, for their
generous help and cooperation. We are particularly grateful to
Mark Thornton and Pauline Weston for acting as principal contacts.

We would also like to thank Exsports, Exeter, for the loan of
several items used in photography.

Designed and typeset by Topics Visual Information, Exeter

Photography by Michael Burton-Pye

Printed in Singapore by Tien Wah Press for
Chansitor Publications Ltd, Norwich

CONTENTS

INTRODUCTION

T he books in this **Faith and Commitment** series give you the chance to look at religions and religious denominations (groups within religions) through the personal reflections of people with a religious commitment.

To create these books, we visited local religious communities in different parts of Britain. We talked to people across the range of ages and roles you'd expect to find in a community – parent, child, grandparent, priest, community worker. That is, we interviewed people like you and your family, your friends, the people where you live. We asked them all the same questions and we've used the themes of those questions as chapter headings in the books.

Each chapter contains extracts from those interviews. People interpret our questions as they want to. They talk freely in their own words about religious ideas and personal experiences, putting emphasis where they think it belongs for them. The result is a set of very individual insights into what religion means to some of the people who practise it. A lot of the insights are spiritual ones, so you may have had similar thoughts and experiences yourself, whether or not you consider yourself a 'religious' person.

You will see that some pages include FACT-FINDER boxes. These are linked to what people say in the interview extracts on these pages. They give you bits of back-up information, such as a definition or where to look up a reference to a prayer or a piece of scripture. Remember that these books are not textbooks. We expect you to do some research of your own when you need to. There are plenty of sources to go to and your teacher will be able to help.

There are also photographs all through the books. Some of the items you can see belong to the people whose interview extracts appear on those pages. Most of these items have personal significance. Some have religious significance, too. They are very special to the people who lent them for particular but different reasons, like special things belonging to you.

Committed to Quakerism: A Christian Community introduces you to ten people who go to the Jesus Lane, Cambridge, Meeting of the Religious Society of Friends. Some go as members of the Society (members are also called Quakers or Friends), others are regular 'attenders' (see page 9). Founded three hundred years ago, the Society of Friends now has about 240 000 members worldwide.

SYLVIA AND BARRY SUTCLIFFE

ABOUT ME

NAME: *Collette W*

WHAT I DO: *I'm eighteen years old, studying for A-levels in French, Economics and Latin at a sixth-form college. I do the exams in about a month and a half's time. After that, I hope to go to university in Aberystwyth to study International Relations.*

Part of the reason why I want to study International Relations is to do with my Quakerism, which was a big influence on my choice of course. But if I'd been going solely for the Quaker approach, there is a course at Bradford University in Peace Studies which would have been the more Quakery one to do. I did actually apply, then plumped for International Relations instead.

SOME OF MY SPECIAL INTERESTS: *I enjoy going to the cinema – a lot – and reading and that sort of stuff. I recently found science fiction.*

MY ROLE IN THE RELIGIOUS COMMUNITY

Generally, I come to the Meeting with my mum. I don't have a specific role, though it's not that I don't feel as if I have a part to play.

You could probably count the number of teenagers in the Meeting on the fingers of one hand, and they usually have Quaker parents. Quakerism is something that people seem to come to a bit later in life. The silence of Meeting doesn't tend to pull young people in. When you've experienced it, you either like it or you don't. I have friends who'll say, 'If I were to go anywhere for religion, it would probably be to the Quakers. But, as a teenager, I don't really do that sort of thing.'

I mean, there's so much going on in our lives that it's almost as if religion takes a back seat. Once you've got to a place where you can feel comfortable with yourself, that's when I think you start looking for God.

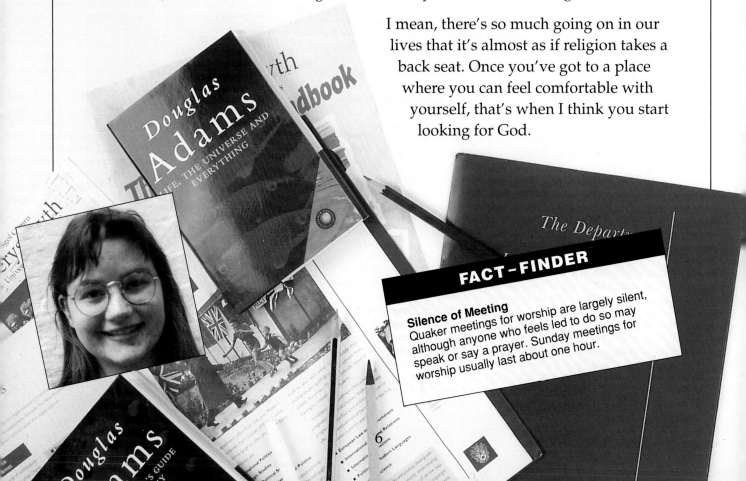

FACT-FINDER

Silence of Meeting
Quaker meetings for worship are largely silent, although anyone who feels led to do so may speak or say a prayer. Sunday meetings for worship usually last about one hour.

NAME: *Pauline W*

WHAT I DO: *I work as a medical secretary. I didn't go back to work until both my children were at secondary school. Tony, my husband, works in community education, specializing in youth work.*

We live out in the country. The garden's huge and has taken over a major part of our lives. Tony's heavily into ponds, so we spend a lot of our time digging out ponds, filling up ponds, digging out weeds, carting weeds about!

Now I'm back at work, my time tends to be totally devoted to running around after everyone else! That's how it seems. But I think really we're a family that shares a lot anyway.

MY FAMILY: *I'm married with two teenage children: Collette's about to take her A-levels, Gavin's in the run-up to GCSE. I thought it was going to be a stressful time for them. I didn't realize how much stress there'd be in it for me as well!*

MY ROLE IN THE RELIGIOUS COMMUNITY: *I'm on the children's committee of the Cambridge Meeting and I've recently been appointed an overseer. I consider myself to be very much a novice overseer. When I was asked if I'd be prepared to do the job, I said, 'I don't know enough to do it.' The others said neither did they when they started. So I thought, 'You could go on for ever thinking you're not ready for this. Unless you take the first step, you'll never get there.'*

FACT-FINDER

Children's committee
Committee responsible for arrangements for children of the Meeting – a crèche and a class for older children – and their interests generally.

Overseer
Overseers together look after the general welfare of all the members and (regular) attenders of the Meeting. They provide practical help for families, children and anyone in special need of support and assistance. They are appointed for three years at a time. (See also page 18.)

THE WATER GARDEN
A complete illustrated guide to creating and planting pools and water features

Water plants

Water lilies

7

NAME: *Emm*

WHAT I DO: *I've just turned twenty-five. I've lived in Cambridge for seven years, except for spending last year in America. At the moment I'm finishing a PhD at the university.*

My research is in philosophy. It involves a lot of searching through archive documents, a lot of headaches and dust! It'll be nice to finish it and get a real job. Personnel work is what I'd like to do, for the inter-personal contact. Having spent two and a half years in a library, I would really like to talk to people again!

SOME OF MY SPECIAL INTERESTS: *I like hill-walking, so I'm in the wrong place for that! I'm learning how to garden but I'm rapidly going off reading, having done so much of it for my studies.*

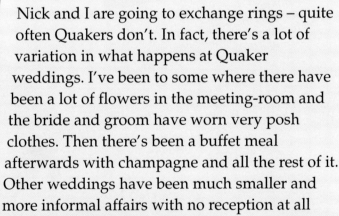

MORE ABOUT ME

This summer I get married to Nick. I'll be married here, in this meeting-house. It should be lovely. One aspect of a Quaker wedding I particularly like is the signing by everybody present of a Quaker marriage certificate. It's not the legal certificate – that's separate. What's very important to me is to have the community witness your marriage in this way and in doing so pledge their support. This means that if you get into any difficulties with your marriage in the future, you can call on anyone who was present to help you work through them.

Nick and I are going to exchange rings – quite often Quakers don't. In fact, there's a lot of variation in what happens at Quaker weddings. I've been to some where there have been a lot of flowers in the meeting-room and the bride and groom have worn very posh clothes. Then there's been a buffet meal afterwards with champagne and all the rest of it. Other weddings have been much smaller and more informal affairs with no reception at all afterwards. Nick and I will be following ours with a folk dance in the evening and simple, self-catered food. That's all we feel would be right.

I'll have to dress up a little for the wedding otherwise the guests will outdress me! It's not a big thing for me. If I see something new that I like, I'll wear that. Otherwise I'll just wear whatever I've got that's cool and pretty. I won't be wearing white!

NAME: *Peter*

WHAT I DO: *I work as a university research fellow in history and archaeology. Basically, I've worked in universities for most of my career.*

MY FAMILY: *I've got a boy, Stephen, who's three years old and we're expecting a second child in July. Stephen's been coming to Meeting since he was about two weeks old – sometimes just for the first quarter of an hour or so. He does seem to sense what's going on, the quietness. Children are important to the meetings. They're certainly not kept quiet all the time or made to spend their time having religious instruction.*

MY ROLE IN THE RELIGIOUS COMMUNITY: *At the moment, I'm what's called an attender of the Cambridge Meeting. People who come to meetings for worship regularly are either attenders or members. Some people apply for membership of the Society of Friends after they've been coming to meetings for only six months or so, others leave it for years and years. Some people stay attenders for life.*

As an attender, you can do most of the things that a member can, and you can have a role in the Meeting. For instance, I help a lot with the crèche for the children. Whether you become a member or not is entirely up to how you feel, whether you're ready to make a commitment to the views and practices of the Society.

SOME OF MY SPECIAL INTERESTS: *I'm very interested in cricket, watching cricket.*

NAME: *Perry*

MY ROLE IN THE RELIGIOUS COMMUNITY: *I'm the librarian for the Cambridge Meeting. We've got a pretty large collection of books here. That's one of my roles.*

I've also been asked to be an elder of the Meeting. The suggestion appalled me to begin with. I thought of an elder as being someone much older, for one thing, with an enormous beard like the Amish elders have in the film "Witness". I thought, 'I'm not like that.' I've accepted the nomination, but I'm going into it not quite sure what my role will be. I think it's going to be more to do with religious education, spiritual education, because that's what fits in most strongly with my interests. I've benefited from some very good teaching myself and that just awakens in me the desire to pass some of it on.

SOME OF MY SPECIAL INTERESTS: *One of my interests is T'ai Chi Ch'uan, Chinese meditative movement. People often refer to it as 'T'ai Chi'. This phrase on its own is sometimes translated as 'supreme ultimate' – the symbol for this is the circular Yin/Yang. 'Ch'uan' means 'fist', and appears in the names of many of the Far East fighting systems. T'ai Chi Ch'uan is actually a martial-arts discipline, although it's practised mostly for health and meditation, which is the way I've studied it.*

I learnt T'ai Chi Ch'uan about fifteen years ago. For me it's part of supporting my Chinese side. I'm actually fully half Chinese. My mother's Chinese and my father's English. I was born and raised in the U.K., so most of my cultural education has been in English. I feel it is important to keep that Chinese side of me alive. It's a great source of strength for me.

WHAT I DO

I'm thirty-five. Up until last year I was working at Cambridge University. My subject was History of Science. I did a science degree first then became very interested in the history of science in its own right. There's a very good department of that here, so I studied History of Science, and ended up teaching it.

I suppose I had ten very happy years studying and teaching History of Science. Then, for the last couple of years it was as if the reason for doing it had suddenly evaporated. Also, I was doing less actual teaching and more administration. At the time doing this had seemed a good move, but it was getting frustrating. So I decided it was time to pull back from that. I was getting a number of very powerful internal signals. One week I remember in particular. On several days in succession, on coming into my office I felt this tremendous sinking of the heart to be back at work. This was very definitely a sign that it was time to move on.

It was at this time that I started thinking about a friend's suggestion that I should go to Woodbrooke, the Quaker Study Centre. Whilst I was still in a job, I was finding it quite difficult to think seriously about what other things I might do. Everything pulled me back to the work I was doing. But some Quaker funding came up, so I left my job, intending to make a complete break, and spent the autumn term at Woodbrooke.

Woodbrooke turned out to be even better than I'd hoped – not only space but a lot of encouragement and stimulation. There are some wonderful teachers there, not so much teachers of facts or knowledge but spiritual teachers.

At Woodbrooke, I was with people from developing countries as well as Quaker development workers who were there together on a course on conflict resolution. I had to face up to the challenge of whether there was something more helpful to others that I could be doing with my life – supporting the weak, the powerless, the underprivileged in the world.

Everybody who works in an academic or teaching environment may be accused of just talking about world problems and not actually doing anything about them. My answer would be that talking *is* a way of changing the world. You can change the way people talk, you can change the way people think. But I must never forget the challenge 'Could I be doing something more helpful?' It's that which will keep the things I think, say and try to teach relevant to the needs and experience and problems of the world.

Now I'm back here in Cambridge, I still hope to work in something to do with education, possibly computer educational resources. I've got a number of job applications in.

FACT-FINDER

Elder
Elders are responsible for caring for the spiritual life of their Meeting and its individual members and (regular) attenders. Elders are appointed for three years at a time. (See also page 18.)

Amish
Group of Baptist Christians in the U.S.A. who use no modern machines or electric power.

NAME: *Colin G*

WHAT I DO: *I'm coming up to fifty-nine years old. Currently I'm a college bursar, although I've worked for almost half of my life in the Civil Service. I'm looking forward to retirement in the next twelve months.*

MY FAMILY: *I've been married to Janet for thirty-five years. I was born into the Society of Friends. Both my parents were in it. My father, like me, was born into it. My mother found it through him, I think.*

SOME OF MY SPECIAL INTERESTS: *A lot of my time and energy is spent on work, but Janet and I go together to the opera two or three times a year. I enjoy going away on holiday. France is a big interest. I don't find it difficult to leave work behind when I have a holiday. I find camping, which we've been doing for the last ten years, particularly relaxing.*

MY ROLE IN THE RELIGIOUS COMMUNITY

I'm one of two joint treasurers to the City-centre Cambridge Meeting. I've been doing that now for three years. I'm more concerned with encouraging people to give than with accounting for the spending – the other treasurer does that. For running the meeting-house and the activities here, we don't need to make a big effort to raise money. That's not to say people are well off. They're not. But there are quite a lot of people and families that can afford to give, and it adds up to enough. The real question is whether we shouldn't as a group also be raising more money than at present to give away to other causes, Quaker and otherwise.

The only big fund-raising drive we've had was ten years ago when we agreed to try to establish a third Meeting in Cambridge. That involved raising a lot of money to buy a building. We didn't have to do that but we decided to. The funds came remarkably easily.

NAME: *Janet G*

MY FAMILY: *I'm married to Colin. We have three children – boy, girl, boy. They're all grown up, all away from home now: one in Edinburgh, one in Egypt and one in Gloucestershire.*

SOME OF MY SPECIAL INTERESTS: *I read a lot, do a bit of painting, do a bit of yoga. I'm going to a portrait class this year. I'm learning Russian. I like opera and music to listen to.*

WHAT I DO

I was a teacher but took early retirement four years ago. There were lots of other things I wanted to do and really there wasn't much time left for teaching! I used to teach maths and do careers advising at one of the sixth-form colleges here. But I'd got stale and there were an awful lot of new things coming up that I really didn't want to be bothered with. So it seemed a good idea to get out.

Now I do a lot of voluntary work: quite a bit for the Cambridge Meeting and for the Society of Friends nationally and also for the Citizen's Advice Bureau and Cambridge Community Mediation Service.

Cambridge Community Mediation Service was set up just a year ago to try to help resolve community disputes, particularly between neighbours. You can take your neighbour to law, but you still have to live next door to them. Very often, whatever the people in dispute say the problem is, what it boils down to is the relationship between them. So we visit each side separately, let them explain the problem as they see it, then bring both sides together. We help them to listen to what each has to say. We don't judge rights and wrongs in any way and we don't find a solution, but we do try to help the two sides find their own solution.

NAME: *Daphne*

MY FAMILY: *My husband and I have had three children, who are now grown up. I became a grandma last September.*

I've just had a family tree given to me, and it shows when my mother became a Quaker. She was twenty. Grandma applied for herself and four of her children, including my mother, to be members of the Society of Friends in 1919.

This was as a direct result of the First World War. Grandma felt out of sympathy with the fighting. In fact, my mother had been involved at that time in befriending the COs – the conscientious objectors – and she ended up marrying one of them. So the Peace Testimony of the Friends has always been part of the fabric of my life.

MY ROLE IN THE RELIGIOUS COMMUNITY

Quakers don't have paid priests – we believe that God can act through any one of us. Everyone has the right to attend our 'business' meetings, called 'meetings for church affairs', and we all take turns at the jobs, when we're asked. I have two at the moment: I'm an elder and an overseer of the Cambridge Meeting.

Overseers have a practical pastoral role. Just this afternoon, I had a phone call from the mother of a mum who is going into hospital on Monday. So I shall go and see if she needs any practical help next week.

Elders take responsibility for Sunday worship, for weddings, funerals and memorial services. I'm an elder appointed to be at our next Quaker wedding so I'm thinking about the couple getting married. Although we don't decide beforehand on a prayer or reading to be used, perhaps I'll think of some suitable words of ministry I might feel called to share, on the day.

This is the lovely thing about my stage of life – I don't have a full-time job,
so I have time to respond when things crop up at short notice. In a busy Meeting
like ours, you need a strong network to keep in touch with people.
I'm happy to be the link person between elders and overseers.
I like the other times when I don't seem to be so busy. That is
when I relax and meditate. These quiet, inwardly listening,
letting-go times help me to be a 'prepared' elder
and overseer.

Daphne HEINE

14

MORE ABOUT ME

When I was seven, my family emigrated to New Zealand. We were met off the boat by Quakers. A lovely Quaker lady took us to her home and tucked us up in bed in a room where you could walk straight out onto a beach by the sea. That sort of kindness has happened to me throughout my life as a Quaker.

'Quaker' is a nickname. Our proper title is the 'Religious Society of Friends'. It is from religious beliefs and practice that this sort of kindness happens to us all, not just to me. This special Quaker friendship is like a family you can walk into anywhere, and find immediate acceptance. It happened to me in New Zealand, in my stays in America, on the Continent, and here in England. I went to Quaker school in New Zealand, a co-educational boarding school, and I found it there. I am lucky I had that experience, to learn Quaker ways and put them into practice.

When I was twenty, I was invited to represent New Zealand at the 1952 World Conference of Friends held in England. Three years later I met my future husband, a Quaker living in New Zealand, who would be travelling to Cambridge to study for his PhD. When we moved to Cambridge, straight away we felt at home in the local Quaker group.

I got involved in the village where we lived, just outside Cambridge. When my children were younger, I helped with the Girl Guide Movement as a Brownie guider for about seven years and as the District Commissioner for five more. Friends believe they should act out their religion, and I've always felt a sense of social responsibility. I was even 'political' and got elected onto the District Council for one term of office.

I don't regard myself as a special person. In fact, I think I'm a very ordinary person, and I feel I've been able to bring an ordinary person's perspective to these jobs. Looking back, I realize that my Quakerism gave me the self-confidence to do them, and it gave me standards. I believe very much that people should be truthful and honest and open and sincere. I think I've got these things from my Quakerism.

FACT-FINDER

Conscientious objectors
People who refuse to join the armed forces on conscience grounds.

Peace Testimony
The important Quaker tradition of acting on the belief that people or nations should never resort to war or violence to 'solve' disputes.

Friends
The Society of Friends or individual members of the Society, i.e. Quakers.

Words of ministry
Anyone present may minister, i.e. say or read something they feel God is telling them to say, during the 'silent' part of a Quaker wedding, or meeting for worship for marriage. (See also page 30.)

NAME: *Rosmarie H*

MY FAMILY: *I was born in Oberdiessbach near Bern in Switzerland in 1933 and trained as a bookseller there. I came to England to work as a bookseller, and that's how I met Robert. We got married in 1958.*

I've got three children. Peter's now thirty-two, Lizzie's thirty-one and David is twenty-seven. They all live away from home. When they were younger, we took them several times to family summer schools at Woodbrooke, which is a Quaker college in Birmingham. These were wonderful. We left it rather late as far as the children were concerned. They were almost teenagers and a bit reluctant to come, but they absolutely loved it. I feel Woodbrooke is home.

SOME OF MY SPECIAL INTERESTS: *Literature is my big love. When I was in my forties, when the children went to school, I did an English degree. I also ran various college libraries for about twelve years.*

MY ROLE IN THE RELIGIOUS COMMUNITY

When we got married, Robert had just joined the Quakers. He wanted us to have a Quaker wedding but to me, coming from Switzerland, where there are very few Quakers, a Quaker wedding seemed very strange. So we were married by a woman friend of mine who was a Swiss minister, living in London.

After we were married, I went to Quaker meetings. When we had children, we brought them along too. I was getting asked to join catering committees, things like that. Then, ten years ago, we were having a celebration here because it was a hundred years since the re-establishing of the Cambridge Meeting. I sat in the meeting-house and realized I'd been part of this community for so long but never actually joined it. When I applied to be a member, people thought I already was one!

Now I'm an overseer for the Cambridge Meeting. I'm also Registering Officer for the Cambridge and Peterborough Monthly Meeting, which covers Cambridge, Peterborough, Huntingdon, Wisbech. Being Registering Officer means I deal with Quaker marriages in this area. I do all the legal work as well as give advice. I was asked to be Registering Officer about five years ago, partly because I used to be a marriage-guidance counsellor. People say it's the best job in the Society because it's the most cheerful one.

A couple who want to get married apply to me first. We meet to talk about their marriage: how they see marriage, what they think marriage is about, whether their views are in sympathy with the Quaker Testimony on Marriage, i.e. that marriage is a commitment under God, hopefully for life. I have to be happy about the marriage going forward. I've got support in this, of course. I can refer to the elders if I need to.

Nowadays the couple themselves may not be Quakers, or perhaps only one of them is, but there should be some commitment to and some link with the Friends. Quaker marriage isn't a service available to the general public. If the bride or groom is not a member of the Society of Friends, they have to talk to two Friends of good standing in their local Meeting and discuss the marriage with them. Hopefully, they'll then get a form signed to say that they are free to go forward to marriage. If there are no objections, the Monthly Meeting then appoints a meeting for worship for the celebration of the marriage. Quaker marriage isn't a special service, it's part of a normal meeting fixed for a special day, usually a Saturday.

On the day itself, I prepare all the legal documents which the couple and their witnesses have to sign. I don't marry the couple; they marry each other. This is important. I don't act as a minister. I'm there only in a legal capacity and to help things along. One thing the couple must do is to keep to the legal form of words when they make their promises. I have to read these aloud.

But, yes, being Registering Officer takes a lot of time. Even after five years, I can get quite tense.

FACT-FINDER

Overseer
Overseers together look after the general welfare of all the members and (regular) attenders of the Meeting. They provide practical help for families, children and anyone in special need of support and assistance. Overseers are appointed for three years at a time.

Monthly Meeting
Quakers may use this term to mean either a group of Quaker Meetings within a particular area or a joint 'business meeting' set up by the group. These meetings for business (formerly held monthly) deal with matters such as applications for membership of the Society of Friends and the appointment of overseers and elders.

Elders
Elders are responsible for caring for the spiritual life of their Meeting and its individual members and (regular) attenders. Elders are appointed for three years at a time. (See also page 18.)

Friends
The Society of Friends or individual members of the Society, i.e. Quakers.

17

NAME: *Robert H*

WHAT I DO: *I retired a year and a half ago from teaching English as a Foreign Language at one of the many language schools in Cambridge.*

SOME OF MY SPECIAL INTERESTS: *My interests? How much time have you got? Art, architecture, geography, languages, music, natural history. I like getting out into the country.*

MY ROLE IN THE RELIGIOUS COMMUNITY

I've been an overseer for the Cambridge Meeting. Now I'm an elder. I felt I didn't cope with being an overseer at all well, although I was probably much too young when I did it. Overseers look after the welfare of the members. There are between ten and a dozen overseers for this Meeting, for example. Each has about twelve to fifteen people that they keep in touch with. Overseer is a role you have for three years or so at a time.

Elders are more concerned with the spiritual side of the Meeting. They are responsible for Sunday meetings for worship. They arrange evening activities – discussion groups and talks, things like that. They take some responsibility in things like funerals, and so on. It doesn't amount to a lot of work. Elders probably have a much lighter task than overseers.

There are no priests, of course, in Quakerism. That's part of the paraphernalia of religion that Quakerism did away with. There were great religious arguments in the seventeenth century, when Quakerism started. Quakers said, 'If people can't agree what a priest should do and what a priest should say and how the priesthood should be passed on, then we won't have priests.'

I personally can't support the idea that priests have special direct access to God or to some sort of individual spiritual inspiration. The wording used in most churches also suggests that God is a power outside you. For a long time, Quakers have said that God is within.

WHERE I BELONG

I belong with the Quakers. I feel at home just walking through the door. That applies not only here at this meeting-house but at other meeting-houses, too. If we're away on holiday and it's a Sunday, we may well go to another meeting-house. I'll feel at home there, relaxed. There's a sense of belonging to a community and being part of a particular spirit. Quakers talk about God being in everyone. When I'm with people who share that belief I feel happy and contented.

PETER

I feel a bit like the court jester at times, as if it's my job to cheer everyone else up. At work, people have been going through difficult times recently, and sometimes I've seemed to be the only one who can see any light at the end of the tunnel.

I don't feel I have any very deep roots to the place where I happen to live. Instead, I feel more like a citizen of the world. I feel strongly that I should be there when those around me need me, and that means being mobile. So I belong with my family and also with anyone else who might need me at any given time.

PAULINE W

I put down roots quite quickly. I've noticed that being a Quaker has helped me do that. For instance, when I moved to Pittsburgh, the only person I knew there was my boyfriend. The first Sunday in Pittsburgh I went to Meeting and immediately I was roped into children's committee work and outreach. So I do start to feel that I belong somewhere pretty quickly.

I feel I belong in Cambridge now because I have enough friends to notice how I am. I think what defines whether I belong somewhere is if other people would notice if I wasn't there. So I definitely belong in Cambridge – the city, not so much my college or university department.

EMM

FACT-FINDER

To Meeting
To a Quaker meeting for worship.

Children's committee
See page 7.

Outreach
Here, helping to make Quaker ideas and contacts easily available so that anyone interested in Quakerism can find out more if they wish to.

L ast week I went to the London Yearly Meeting. Our main task this year was to agree revisions to what's called the *Book of Discipline*. Part of it sets out the Quaker position on Christian faith and practice and part of it is about how the Society of Friends is run.

Once every generation (about every twenty-five years), the *Book of Discipline* gets revised. Before the Yearly Meeting this summer, we'd had a draft – a revision committee had been working on it for the last seven years. What the Yearly Meeting had to do was agree a final revised version and accept it, 'own' it. This had to be done in front of seven hundred people, which was an incredible exercise.

I was very moved by how that meeting went. There's an enormous breadth of view in Quakerism now. Some Quakers' beliefs are centred on Christ, other Quakers are universalist. This means there is potential for conflict. But there was so much love flowing at that meeting, partly from the Clerks who were running it. That's what stays with me. We got rather stuck on the issue of personal relationships, so when sexuality came up on the agenda the Clerk said, 'Dear Friends, we need to be very tender with each other on this.' That sort of attitude to each other made me feel I was in the right place.

I think I would find another church a bit too formal now and very concerned with externals. I like the Quaker simplicity, honesty and truthfulness. Not too much external show. No keeping up with the Joneses, which is such a relief. Although not everybody manages to be loving all the time, at least people are trying.

I like the insistence on equality. I like the way that at least the idea that women are equal has been part of Quakerism from the very beginning, and women are certainly equal now. At the London Yearly Meeting, the Clerk and the Assistant Clerk were women, and they were excellent. I think it's one of the most responsible things you can do in the Society, to be Clerk to the Yearly Meeting.

FACT-FINDER

London Yearly Meeting
Any member of the Society of Friends who belongs to a Quaker Meeting in England, Scotland or Wales may take part in this annual gathering. Each Monthly Meeting (see page 17) in these countries makes sure at least one of their members goes to London Yearly Meeting. This is the final policy/decision-making body for Quakers in England, Scotland and Wales. The words are also used to mean all Quakers in mainland Britain. (Quakers in Ireland have their own Yearly Meeting.)

Book of Discipline
Its full title is *Book of Christian Discipline of London Yearly Meeting of the Religious Society of Friends*.

Universalist
These Quakers believe that guidance and inspiration from God are accessible to people of any religion or none and that no faith can claim to have a 'monopoly of truth'.

Peace Testimony
The important Quaker tradition of acting on the belief that people or nations should never resort to war or violence to 'solve' disputes.

Anglican • Swiss Reformed Church Methodist • German Lutheran Church
Names of four (Protestant) Christian denominations. There are many similarities between these churches as well as some significant differences.

I find the Peace Testimony quite difficult. I grew up next door to Germany during the Second World War, and I don't think I could have been a pacifist at that time.

But I do miss the music, I miss the literature you get in, let's say, an Anglican Sunday service.

I think if I had stayed in Switzerland I would still be a member of the Swiss Reformed Church. When I came to England, I tried going to the Methodists and the Anglicans and the German Lutheran Church, but it was very unsatisfactory with Robert happily settled at the Cambridge Meeting and me flitting about. But I feel that being a Quaker suits me in my uncertain state. I do find, as I get older, that things don't get any more certain – rather disappointingly.

ROSMARIE S.

Geographically, I'm not sure where I belong. I was born in Wales but was very conscious there that my family wasn't Welsh. After getting married, I spent the next fifteen years in Scotland, where I felt very Scottish but always knew that actually I wasn't. Now I'm in England, and although I really am English, parts of me feel as if they should belong in Wales or Scotland!

Spiritually, I belong in the Society of Friends. I was born and brought up a Quaker. We've got a family tree that goes back to the seventeenth century and it shows that my mother's family were Quakers. As children, we were taken to Meeting and I've always felt very much at home at Meeting, wherever that's been. At Meeting, I know I'm always on the same wavelength as the people there. When I talk to them I'll find we have the same sort of values and often similar interests. I know I've got a right to be there. I don't have to prove myself or establish my position. I belong, and that's that.

FACT-FINDER

To Meeting
To meetings for worship at a Quaker meeting-house.

Values
Ideas about what is right, what is wrong, what is of real value in life and how people should behave.

Particularly as a woman, I've always felt comfortable with Quakerism. There's never been any hassle. No one thinking a woman's place is in the home or that women shouldn't have a role in running things. I've always had an active part in Quaker affairs and felt this was acceptable and right.

JANET G.

I was brought up an Anglican, and when I finished National Service I thought I might go in for the priesthood. I applied to be trained as an Anglican priest, but the college suggested I got an 'ordinary' job for a while first. However, after doing a languages degree, I started teaching English in a language school in Cambridge.

At that time, my beliefs were all based on a terribly frail set of ideas I had. I didn't really know any theology, not properly. I think for quite a long time I was uncertain just what my ideas were. There were so many things I simply couldn't be sure about. Jesus, after all, had lived nearly two thousand years ago, and the Gospels had inconsistencies and were open to various interpretations. Evidently, something rather significant seemed to have happened at Pentecost, but I found it very difficult to judge what. I'd become increasingly disillusioned with ideas like atonement – one person, Jesus, dying so that other people's sins could be forgiven. This idea seemed extraordinary to me, it didn't make any sense.

I've always had a lot of contact with overseas people, as a student and then in my work. I remember someone persuading a Sri Lankan friend of mine to go to a gathering being held by some Christian group which was visiting Cambridge. Next day, I asked him how it had gone, and he was very angry. He said he'd been told that the only way he could be saved was by becoming a Christian. He was a Buddhist himself. He insisted this couldn't be right, and I had to agree with him. I've always thought of that moment as a turning-point. Other religions couldn't be discounted just like that.

Later, an Indian friend was invited to a Quaker meeting. He asked whether I'd like to go with him, and I was quite intrigued by what I found. But I didn't go back immediately. I suppose there was a gap of about a year. In the meantime, other things began to get a little clearer. When I did go back, it felt right. Four years later, about the time Rosmarie and I got married, I applied for membership of the Society of Friends.

Within Quakerism, there's a huge range of belief. Some Quakers talk about Jesus giving them their guiding principles. He was obviously a person who had tremendous religious insights. He seems to have had the power of healing, and there are a lot of stories about that. But I've always found the claim that he is the Son of God an obstacle. It puts Christianity in a superior position to other faiths, which I find difficult to accept.

ROBERT H

FACT-FINDER

Anglican
Member of the worldwide Anglican church, which includes the Church of England.

National Service
From 1945 to 1960, all young men in the U.K. had to spend two years serving in the armed forces unless they registered officially as conscientious objectors. That is, as refusing to join the armed forces on conscience grounds.

Theology
Ideas/theories about God and religion based on reasoning and scholars' research.

Gospels
The four books in the Bible containing accounts of Jesus' life and teaching.

Pentecost
Here, the day when Jesus' followers were filled with God's Holy Spirit according to the account in Acts 2 in the Bible.

Sins
Behaviour that is wrong, i.e. that breaks God's rules.

Saved
Here, saved from punishment by God for (his) sins.

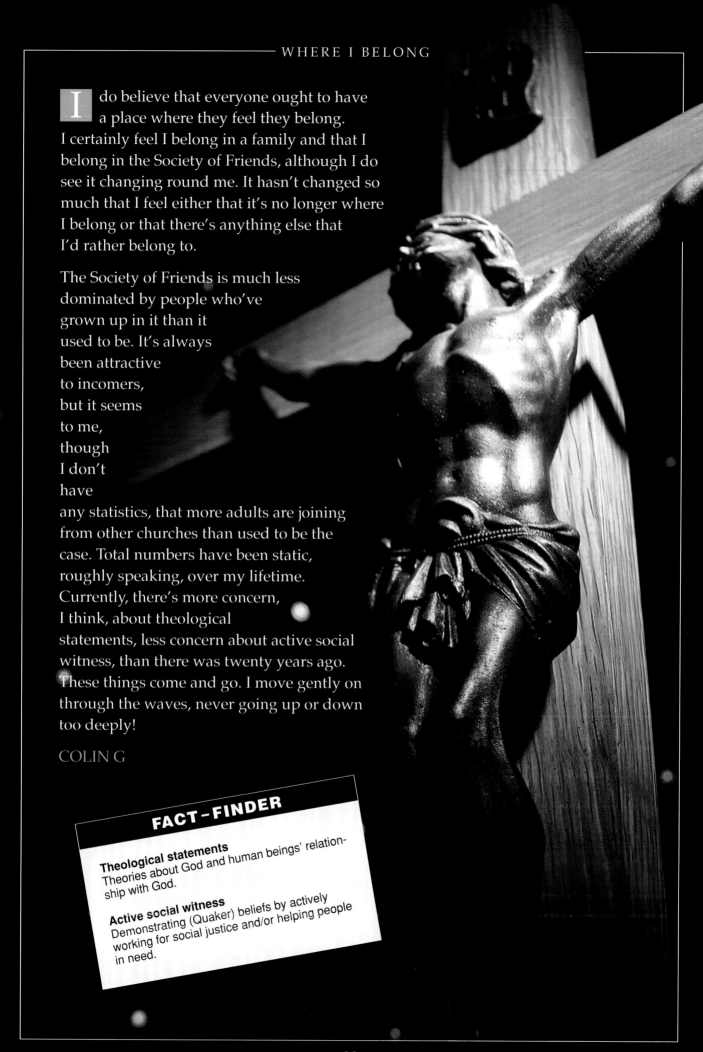

I do believe that everyone ought to have a place where they feel they belong. I certainly feel I belong in a family and that I belong in the Society of Friends, although I do see it changing round me. It hasn't changed so much that I feel either that it's no longer where I belong or that there's anything else that I'd rather belong to.

The Society of Friends is much less dominated by people who've grown up in it than it used to be. It's always been attractive to incomers, but it seems to me, though I don't have any statistics, that more adults are joining from other churches than used to be the case. Total numbers have been static, roughly speaking, over my lifetime. Currently, there's more concern, I think, about theological statements, less concern about active social witness, than there was twenty years ago. These things come and go. I move gently on through the waves, never going up or down too deeply!

COLIN G

FACT-FINDER

Theological statements
Theories about God and human beings' relationship with God.

Active social witness
Demonstrating (Quaker) beliefs by actively working for social justice and/or helping people in need.

FACT-FINDER

In Meeting
In Quaker meetings for worship and/or among the people there.

I feel I belong in Meeting and I feel I belong with my family. I don't actually feel a geographical sense of belonging in any one place. We moved to where we live now from Suffolk when I was eleven. I went to the village school for a term, then to a secondary school in a nearby town. Any roots I had to the village sort of shrivelled at that point.

When I'm at a particular school, I do feel as if I belong there. But my secondary school didn't have a sixth form, so I've now had to move on. Already I feel I've lost touch with the secondary school. It's almost as if where I am at the present time is where I belong. I can't say that a particular town or village or whatever is home, but I've always felt I could walk into any meeting-house anywhere and feel that I belong there.

COLLETTE W

I first started finding out about Quakers about ten years ago, when I shared a flat with a Quaker. I thought at that time that if I was going to join any religious group, it would be the Quakers. But I didn't feel the need.

It was about five years later that I began to realize that religious things, spiritual things, were something I couldn't do on my own – I had to be part of a community. So I started attending my first Quaker meetings. From a very early stage, I felt that the Quaker tradition was one I wanted to know and be part of. So I definitely feel that where I belong is within the Quaker community from a religious point of view.

I also think my role in life is as an educator or teacher of some kind. That's where I think my gifts lie.

PERRY

WHAT I FEEL STRONGLY ABOUT

I think one of the things I feel most strongly about is truth. I don't just mean truth in the sense of a fact being true or false. I also mean truth as something which is right and appropriate.

What hurts me is when I see discussions about education or politics or social relations getting completely bogged down in some out-of-the-way point. I think, 'That's not where the centre is. It's a diversion.' Sometimes it's done as straightforward, calculated deception or bafflement, particularly in public politics. Sometimes it's an unconscious psychological defence, in which case I hope I'm more inclined to be tender. If someone's got defences that powerful then there's probably a very good reason for them.

Some of the early Quakers in the seventeenth century referred to themselves as 'publishers of truth'. I'd like to think of myself as a publisher of truth. I used to say to my university students, 'A thing being true isn't a sufficient reason for saying it.' I'd get essays from them full of perfectly true facts, but were they important or alive? A telephone directory is true, on the whole, but who gives a monkey's? So in my direct, personal teaching, if I've done anything useful, it's been helping students see past the facts and the knowledge which they've been accumulating, to the core. Bringing the truth out like that is part of publishing the truth. When it's right, you know it's right – it shines with its own light, it works with its own power.

PERRY

I feel strongly about an awful lot of things: the Peace Testimony, social justice and all the things that go with that. I've tried in a number of ways to put these into practice over the years. I've always accepted in principle that the Peace Testimony is important. But for a long time it never really touched me because it didn't require me to take any decisions. When I was growing up, for instance, boys in the Meeting were still being conscripted. They had to decide whether or not to take alternative service, as my husband did and my brother did. But I didn't have to make that choice, so I never thought out what my position would be.

It was really only in the 1980s, when CND was revitalized, that I got involved with the Peace Movement. My daughter was about sixteen at the time. She and a Dutch girl who was staying with us wanted to go up to a big demonstration being planned for Trafalgar Square. I was a bit unsure about it but said I was happy for them to go if they wanted to. Then my daughter asked, 'Why aren't you coming?' I thought, 'Well, why aren't I?' After that, I went on several more demonstrations and became an active member of the local CND group in Cambridge. I started a Teachers for Peace group in Cambridge, went as a member of that to the USSR, and got pretty heavily involved in peace activities. So I suppose working for peace has been my big thing in recent years.

But I've always felt strongly about social justice generally. My work with the Citizen's Advice Bureau and with homeless and disadvantaged people is about that. Earlier, it was a sense of social responsibility that drew me into teaching in the first place.

JANET G

FACT-FINDER

Peace Testimony
The important Quaker tradition of acting on the belief that people or nations should never resort to war or violence to 'solve' disputes.

Conscripted
Called up for compulsory service in the armed forces.

Alternative service
Young men who were conscripted could ask to serve in a non-combatant unit or do medical or agricultural work. See opposite.

CND · Peace Movement
The Campaign for Nuclear Disarmament (founded in 1958) played an important role in the growing movement working for world peace at that time.

I feel strongly about pacifism. I think pacifism has provided me with an opportunity to express conviction by doing things which I'm less keen to try to express in words or argument. For example, a crucial thing for young men of my generation was being faced at eighteen with National Service. My brother didn't find it a problem and went into the RAF. He'd drifted away from Quakerism as a teenager. I did find it a problem. So I registered as a conscientious objector and served in the Friends Ambulance Unit International Service for two years. I'm currently Treasurer for the Trustees of the Friends Ambulance Unit.

I feel strongly that, when one is expressing deepest feelings, what is more important and more reliable than words is behaviour. For me and I think for quite a lot of people, our words can often outstrip what we're able to do. It's not that I believe behaviour is always reliable. Most of us would, I hope, wish to behave in ways that are better than those we normally achieve. However I do feel strongly that words without action are not empty exactly, but they're only part of the story, and a small part, really.

COLIN G

FACT-FINDER

National Service • Conscientious objector
From 1945 to 1960, all young men in the U.K. had to spend two years serving in the armed forces unless they registered officially as conscientious objectors. That is, as refusing to join the armed forces on conscience grounds.

Friends Ambulance Unit
Quaker organization founded during the First World War as a non-combatant service which any conscientious objector could join instead of the armed services. Work done by the FAU included caring for wartime casualties and refugees.

I feel strongly about social justice. Social justice is important to Quakers, so it's not surprising to find Quakers active in charities or pressure groups, things like that. For instance, because of my views about social justice, I'm active in politics. I'm a member of the Labour Party. I feel particularly strongly at the moment about poverty in our society. So there's an overlap between my spiritual life as a Quaker and other things I feel motivated to do. But the link between them is one I make myself.

PETER

There are two areas of social action that I often wonder whether I'm doing enough about or whether I'm aware enough of the issues. One is the well-being of the planet, the other is social justice for humans. I found an interesting series of Quaker work-shops on *Justice, Peace and the Integrity of Creation* which look at how problems like pollution and poverty are interconnected. But if I only had a limited amount of time or money, my priorities would be first the well-being of the planet and then, when that's taken care of, its people, locally then globally – especially issues like homelessness and unfair distribution of resources.

I've taken part in some Greenpeace demonstra-tions and support Greenpeace financially. I also support Friends of the Earth and get involved in recycling campaigns and composting campaigns and all that sort of stuff. I did contemplate volunteering for the Winter Comfort Bus which gives out food and drink every day to homeless people on the streets of Cambridge. But I didn't feel I could cope with the despair of the people who go there. For Amnesty International, I write letters. Again, I feel that's all I can do. I don't have the nerve to confront anyone face to face.

EMM

There's just this one thing. Quakers say that there's something of God in every man and every woman. That's important to me. We're so inclined to pigeon-hole people: these people are worth more than these, for example. I really do think that in the eyes of God we're all the same. He loves us all. We're worthwhile because he loves us.

I don't always remember that in everything I do. But I feel the justice of it very strongly.

ROSMARIE H

I feel strongly about intolerance and prejudice, whether it's prejudging a personality or a situation or whatever. Everyone has a right to their own view. I don't necessarily have to agree with it, but it's not my place to judge it.

PAULINE W

I feel strongly about racialism. I am *very* concerned about racial equality and respect for those of other races (as I am for those of other faiths).

ROBERT H

I feel strongly about a lot of things! I feel strongly about how youth is portrayed in the media at the moment. I find it infuriating when newspapers give the impression that anyone between the ages of, say, fourteen and twenty-three must be going out every night taking drugs, joy-riding, you name it. There are a substantial number of us teenagers out there who don't do drugs, don't go around stealing or joy-riding. People whose only image of young people is through the media must be lumping us all into a pretty distorted picture.

I also feel strongly about what's going on in the world. I was watching 'Cry Freedom!' on television the other day. The first full South African elections had just happened, and watching the film it really hit me, what had been achieved in South Africa. You see things going on in the world – war in Bosnia, riots in L.A. Suddenly here was something I could point to and say, 'This is a good thing that's happened. This is something going right. Something you can grab on to. Something you can use as a symbol that the world is getting a little bit better.' OK, it's one country and one election. Who knows what's going to happen in the future? But for that moment on that day, there was good news.

COLLETTE W

FACT-FINDER

Cry Freedom!
This Richard Attenborough film gives a vivid picture of the struggle against apartheid in South Africa.

First full South African elections
The first national elections at which all (adult) South Africans could vote, whatever their colour or race.

MY FAVOURITE FESTIVAL

F estivals aren't important to Friends and we don't celebrate them. We're a tradi-
tional Quaker family that doesn't keep dates and seasons. So it's difficult to know
what to say about festivals, which sounds as if Quakers aren't very good at celebrating.
I suppose, in a way, that's true. We do have quite a lot of fun together, though – at
weekend gatherings, like conferences.

My favourite Quaker celebration would be the service for marriage. I've always loved
Quaker weddings. My own was lovely, so was my daughter's. Somebody at
my daughter's wedding who wasn't a Friend got it right, I
think, when they said afterwards, 'That was lovely. I
felt I really was a part of it.' Sometimes when I go to a
church wedding, I feel I'm a spectator. But at a
Quaker wedding everyone participates.

FACT-FINDER

Friends
Members of the Society of Friends, i.e.
Quakers.

At the beginning, the couple make their promises.
After that, it's a normal meeting for worship, which
means that anyone may speak who feels moved to do
so. Usually a lot of people do. You hear
some very nice, straight-
forward anecdotes
about what
the couple have
done but also thoughts
about marriage and deeper
things as well. Then, at the end,
there's a large certificate that everyone
signs. When I look at my certificate, there are
signatures from everyone who was at my wedding,
including the children, and I can remember them all.

JANET G

M arriage, to me, is an extraordinarily important and quite moving occasion. It's a
festival for everyone who's there. For me, it involves memories of my own
wedding and marriage, a renewal of my commitment, hopes for the new marriage. It's a
chance to take stock and a chance to renew, which is, I suppose, the general spirit of many
festivals. But the celebration is about people I know and experiences I've had, rather than
some distant event in the Bible. This is important to my way of looking at things.

COLIN G

Quakers have meetings for special purposes, and one which I find particularly powerful and moving is our memorial meeting. It's a Quaker funeral. Obviously, people who come to a Quaker funeral bring with them a complex mass of emotions. But in amongst all that there is a strong focus on thanksgiving for the person's life. This comes through in the way that memorial meetings are conducted. The type of contribution I find most moving is when people remember the person's life and all the good things about it.

Alongside this is another Quaker tradition: writing what are called 'testimonies' after a well-known Quaker person has died. They're like obituaries, except that they're not obituaries. Their full title is 'A testimony to the grace of God as shown in the life of ...'. Their aim, which sometimes comes across very well indeed, is to say that these are the features of this Friend's life in which we can see the grace of God working. That to me is a very important thing.

Different people have different views about whether there's life after death. One thing which I've found very powerful and positive about Quakerism is that there's always emphasis laid on *this* life, the here and now. For me, that's very important. If we're going to find our salvation, if we're going to find the Kingdom of Heaven, I want to do it now. If we can't do it now, I can't see that the existence of a life after death is necessarily going to help. If you can't become reconciled, whole, entire, living in the spirit while you're alive, are things going to be any easier when you're dead? So the way we conduct our memorial meetings seems to me to put priorities the right way round.

PERRY

FACT-FINDER

Grace of God
Here, God's goodness, inspiration or power.

Salvation
Escape from the power of (one's own) sin (wrongdoing).

Kingdom of Heaven
Literally, the Kingdom of God, where God rules.

I wasn't born into Quakerism, so it doesn't seem strange to me to recognize Christian festivals. I don't have such strong feelings about them as I used to, though. I think it's nice to join in with other people celebrating at these times, and I don't see any reason why I shouldn't be taking part. So for the last year or two on Christmas Eve I've been to Midnight Mass at our local parish church. That's something I actually didn't do before I became a Quaker.

Christmas is my favourite festival. That's partly because, ever since I was a child, I've always felt a special peace arrive on Christmas Eve. As a child, I always thought that that peace would stay, and that people would go on behaving just as they did at Christmas. But it didn't happen.

PAULINE W

FACT-FINDER

Midnight Mass ...
Like many other Anglican churches, Pauline's local parish church holds a special Eucharist starting very late on Christmas Eve to celebrate the birth of Jesus.

Specific day ...
On Good Friday, many Christians attend special services remembering how Jesus died. Christians believe that Jesus died to save people from their sins (wrongdoing).

A s a family we celebrate Christmas – Christmas dinner, turkey, presents, Christmas tree, the whole shebang. We go to grandparents. It's a family day.

The last couple of years, Mum and Dad have gone to Midnight Mass at our village church. I went two years ago but it wasn't for me. It didn't feel right. So, personally, I don't go out and look for religious celebrations to take part in. But going to Meeting round about Christmas, there is a definite change of tone, even though Quaker Meetings don't celebrate Christmas. It's obvious that Christmas is in our thoughts. We're holding it in our hearts rather than going around saying, 'Hey, it's Christmas!'

I think the fact that Quakers don't make a great deal out of festivals is because we hold certain important things in our hearts every day of the year. If you hold it in your heart, there's no need to have a specific day to remember that Jesus died on the cross so that everyone could be saved. You've been doing that for the whole of your life.

COLLETTE W

C hristmas has no particular religious significance for me. We cannot say when or even at what time of the year Jesus was born. The stories in the Gospels about the wise men and the shepherds are probably myths. But I enjoy the music. I can just about play the piano, and before Christmas I sit down and try to play a few of the lesser-known carols. We create a lovely atmosphere at home. We have a tree with candles which we light on Christmas Eve. There's a very pleasant, warm feeling about it all.

ROBERT H

I feel that festivals should be celebrated, and we do celebrate them in our family. Christmas Day is always a magical time, especially with children. We celebrate it at home like everyone else. As far as its meaning is concerned, I have to say that I'm not sure about the literal story of Christmas. But, as someone said at a meeting, you can believe in Christmas for Christmas Day, at least.

Here, we have a meeting for worship on Christmas Day, whether it falls on a Sunday or not. The meeting isn't different to other times of the year – it's still the same format, still quiet – except that we do have some music beforehand. People sit quietly and listen to the music. If there's any ministry in the meeting, it usually mentions Christmas.

Normally, there's no music in Meeting because it distracts. At Quaker meetings, quite often you're thinking about other people. These can be people you know quite well. Perhaps they have a problem, though that's obviously not the only reason for thinking of someone else. I think quite a lot of people sit in Meeting not always for the spiritual experience but because it gives them a chance to think about other people and about issues and so on. Music would be a distraction to that.

PETER

FACT-FINDER

Literal story of Christmas
Peter means that he's not sure whether or not the sections in the Bible about Jesus' birth describe actual historical events.

Ministry
During a meeting for worship, anyone present may 'minister', i.e. say or read anything they feel God is telling them to say.

A
SPECIAL MOMENT

T ony and I weren't Quakers when we got married. Our wedding was an Anglican one. The church where we were married was set in woodland and, because it was April, all the daffodils were out. We were outside the church having our photographs taken surrounded by daffodils – it was really quite magical – and raindrops started to fall.

The year before I'd been in America. A little Jewish boy called Davy had asked, 'Are you and Tony going to get married?'
I'd said, 'Yes, I hope so.'
'In that case,' he said, 'I hope it rains on your wedding day.'
'Thank you very much, Davy,' I said, 'that's lovely!'
'No,' he said, 'in our religion it's good luck if it rains on your wedding day.'

When those raindrops started falling, I thought of Davy and his good luck. That was a very special moment.

PAULINE W

FACT-FINDER

Anglican
Name of a worldwide Christian denomination which includes the Church of England.

I've had a few of what you might call epiphanies. Little ones. I remember being at Woodbrooke sitting in a meeting for worship and seeing my daughter Lizzie, about seventeen then, walking past the window with a baby in her arms. The garden was behind her and the sun shone through them. It was just wonderful, a moment of transcendence.

I remember sitting in a case discussion when I training to be a marriage-guidance counsellor. I found that all very hard. I don't think I really wanted to do it, although I kept passing at each stage. I was sitting there and thinking, 'I can't do this. I just don't want to do this. How can I tell these nice people that I don't want to do it?'

Suddenly, I heard an inner voice saying, 'You've never really said yes to this, have you?' Just like that, out of the blue. Nothing world shaking, but very clear. I thought, 'That's right, I haven't. That's the problem.' I don't know where that voice came from, but it made a difference. It changed my whole attitude. When my tutor went through my next set of case notes, she said, 'What's happened to you?'

ROSMARIE H

FACT-FINDER

Epiphanies
Manifestations (appearances or showings) of God. The Christian Feast of the Epiphany (on 6 January) commemorates the showing of Jesus to the wise men.

Woodbrooke
Quaker college in Birmingham. Rosmarie and her family used to attend summer schools there.

Moment of transcendence
A feeling or experience somehow beyond or surpassing material things.

When Stephen was born – that was special. I know it's probably a fairly obvious example, but it was quite difficult to believe that something quite like that was actually happening.

PETER

T he first time I went to Junior Yearly Meeting I was just about to turn sixteen. This meeting is a conference for sixteen to eighteen year olds from all over the country. It lasts for about five days, and there's a theme, and workshops, and small group discussions, outside speakers and lots of fun time.

That year there were about a hundred and fifty of us. On the first evening we had a meeting for worship late at night after the initial getting-to-know-you games. We didn't have appointed elders and we didn't have a clock in the room. We sat in circles around candles. The meeting went on for two hours. It didn't feel like two hours.

That was the first time I'd experienced knowing I was in a gathered meeting. It still stands out for me as a special moment. It's the birth of my commitment to Quakerism. Six months later I joined the Society.

I'd been an attender for six years before that. I was in a very small Meeting that was largely of older people. I felt welcome, but I didn't quite know what was going on. But at the Junior Yearly Meeting, I was definitely part of it, and part of what made it work.

EMM

FACT-FINDER

Elders
Elders are appointed to care for the spiritual life of a particular Quaker Meeting and are responsible for Sunday meetings for worship.

Gathered meeting
Meeting for worship where, without saying anything, the people present all feel they are thinking along the same lines and are all feeling God's presence. (See also page 38.)

Attender
Someone who regularly attends Quaker meetings but has not yet become a member of the Society of Friends.

M y mother's funeral was a special event. She died about eight years ago now. She'd had a good life but she was failing. There was no question that it wasn't very satisfying and complete that she'd come to the end of her life.

The funeral was quite complicated to organize. After the cremation, we'd arranged to have a meeting for worship in the meeting-house where my mother had worshipped in Swindon. I remember this tremendous feeling of: 'It's over to you, God. This is one stage I don't have to worry about. It's all in good hands. I can sit back and let it happen now.'

JANET G

I went to a conference a couple of years ago. I was part of an English group, and there was a German group and a Croatian group. On the last night we had an international entertainments evening when each group did their own thing.
Our group did morris dancing – this was typifying our country! – with silly things dangling off our trousers. The Croatian group did folk songs and some rather deep and meaningful sketches about the UN's role in Yugoslavia. Then the lights went down, and there was the German group sitting with lighted candles, singing 'Heal the World'. Everyone in the room was singing it. That was a special moment. We were all thinking the same thing and wanting the same thing. There was a unity of purpose which really felt good.

COLLETTE W

FACT-FINDER

UN's role in Yugoslavia
United Nations troops were sent in 1992 to help deliver food and other humanitarian aid to victims of fighting in the former Yugoslavia between, mainly, Bosnians, Croats and Serbs. Much argument followed over what else they could or should be doing to help bring about peace there.

Heal the World
From Michael Jackson's album 'Dangerous'.

WORDS THAT MEAN A LOT TO ME

Words are important. When the right words are used, they give you something to latch on to. They can stay with you for a long time.

Sometimes, at a meeting for worship, the ministry can be just a couple of sentences long but it stays with you for ever. Or someone may say a lot but really it comes across as a bit of a jumble and doesn't mean a great deal. It's interesting how often, though, the things that are said at meetings – especially the shorter things – manage to express a shared feeling or a shared idea and strike a chord with a thought that's going through your own mind.

PAULINE W

FACT-FINDER

Ministry
Here, what is said, by anyone present.

S ome Quakers say a lot in Meeting. Others have been to Meeting all their lives and never said a word – not during the meeting for worship itself. You can contribute by being quiet. There's no pressure to say anything. Whether you say anything or how much you say isn't particularly relevant.

In fact, the special meetings are often the ones which are completely silent, when people don't say or read out anything. Sometimes Quakers will refer to a meeting being 'gathered together'. This means that, without saying anything, the people present feel they are thinking along the same lines. You can't predict what's going to happen at a meeting. You don't come to a meeting expecting anything is going to happen. But people seem to know when something has happened.

There have been some meetings when we've sat in silence for an hour and although nothing has happened it's been good. At other times we've been silent throughout but the meeting hasn't been 'gathered' for some reason.

PETER

Q uakers place a great emphasis on silence. Not merely as the absence of words but the silence which comes before the word and the silence which comes after the word. Not empty silence either but a silence full of possibilities. I've been in meetings for worship which have started in silence, and you can sense the possibilities. Then someone speaks, and the words come out of the silence and go back into the silence afterwards.

We have a phrase in our *Book of Discipline* about being open to new light from wherever it may come. Speaking for myself, I'm one of those Quakers who are not anchored to any particular text, like the Bible. I use the Bible as a powerful source of inspiration, but not as an authority. Many works of fiction are equally important to me – the novels of the American writer Ursula Le Guin, for instance, and particularly her novel *The Dispossessed*, which I suppose indirectly made me a Quaker before I was one. Those are words to which I return.

FACT-FINDER

Book of Discipline
See page 20.

PERRY

Q uakers like worship based on silence. We like to let words go. We distrust words. We tend to think they're not meaningful until we've made them meaningful by living out what we say. So words don't come that easily to us.

DAPHNE

T he short answer is: I don't respond through words, really.

COLIN G

S omething which has kept me going is a sense of the grace of God. It kept me going even when I had post-natal depression and I wasn't aware of much else that was happening. It's a sort of assurance. The words are less important than what they're trying to describe, but 'the grace of God' – whatever that may mean – is something I'm very aware of.

As far as actual words are concerned, I love the Psalms, especially the first part of Psalm 139.

ROSMARIE H

FACT-FINDER

Grace of God
Possible meanings include goodness, mercy, kindness, favour, goodwill, help, inspiration of/from God.

Psalms
The Book of Psalms in the Bible is a very ancient collection of sacred songs or hymns still used today by both Christians and Jews.

I think words do matter, but I think too much emphasis is probably placed on set forms of words – like at the Anglican Midnight Mass I went to. There the priest at the front said something and the people replied in their set ways. It seems to me that to truly mean something, words should come from your heart, from your soul. They're worth more than words you rattle off because you've learnt them.

Words are also worth more if they're expressing ideas and thoughts that you're able to put into practice. It's all very well saying, 'I am a pacifist', for example. But the words themselves aren't worth a great deal if you can't back them up.

FACT-FINDER

Anglican Midnight Mass
See page 32.

Soul
The innermost part of a person.

Words are important. They have the power to affect everyone, really. Words – a speech by Mandela, for instance, or Churchill or Hitler – have the power to do an awful lot, for good and for evil.

COLLETTE W

W ords matter, and cause a lot of trouble sometimes. A lot of differences between people are over using words and meaning different things by them. One of the big differences amongst Friends at the moment is about words. A lot of Friends find difficulty in describing themselves as Christian.

I'm perfectly happy calling myself Christian. Christ is important in my life. I follow Jesus' teaching and feel he gave us an example of how God wants us to live. I also feel no worry at all about saying that I don't believe Jesus was divine. I don't believe Jesus thought he was divine, the Son of God. I don't know what happened at the Resurrection and that doesn't really bother me very much either. I feel I don't have to decide whether I believe in these things in order to call myself a Christian. But using a word like 'Christian' is a tremendous barrier to some Quakers, because they feel it implies things they don't believe.

JANET G

FACT-FINDER

Friends
Members of the Society of Friends, i.e. Quakers.

Resurrection
Rising (of Jesus) from the dead.

I t's particular phrases that mean a lot to me. For instance, 'That of God in every person', which comes from George Fox, is one I often think about. What does it mean? Where would God be? What does that tell me about the nature of God? Is God something outside people? Or between people?

Then there's 'Disciple in the school of Christ'. This is how some Quakers understand Christianity at the moment (being a disciple in the school of Christ, learning from his example). The man I'm about to marry is an Anglican with a very clear idea of who Christ was. I've never had that. I was put off Anglican and Methodist Christianity at school. For a long time, the word 'Christ' was a no-no for me. If anyone used it, I'd just switch off. I couldn't handle it. But now, over the last three years, I've started to understand the role of Christ in my life. That phrase, 'Disciple in the school of Christ', has helped.

EMM

FACT-FINDER

George Fox (1624–1691)
Preacher born in Leicestershire who was the main founder of the Quaker movement.

Anglican • Methodist
Names of two worldwide Christian denominations or churches.

God is love. It's a rather trite-sounding, overworked expression, and for a long time I used to wonder what it meant. Then one day, I realized that 'God is love' is an exact description. God to me is a loving power which we all have.

It's a power which can be focused on another person. Perhaps someone is in a difficult position. Perhaps they have a hard decision to make, or they're distressed or there's tension between them and others. It's possible to focus on that person or those people very intensely in a loving way with no words. I have seen the results. Quite a number of times the person appears to have been helped. It's almost like faith-healing – nothing to do with ill health, but responding to people with some kind of need. I think they can be prayed for with this focusing of love.

I find I have to visualize someone to be able to pray for them. I can't really pray for people I've not met. Sometimes, you see notices saying: 'Pray for so-and-so in prison somewhere in Latin America.' I couldn't do that in any sort of meaningful way. So prayer is limited in what it can do. I don't think you can pray about the weather. I don't think you can pray for someone to pass an exam, although you can pray for them to be calm and collected and in the right frame of mind to do their best. I think an awful lot of prayers, particularly those said in the churches, are about things you can't pray about at all.

So, as I see it, what has been called God is this power to love, which is in everybody. It's there all the time, and you don't need to go to a special place to show it. I don't think God exists as a person nor that God is the creator of the world. God is a power human beings have developed during their evolution: it's an increased consciousness. To me, it makes all faiths equally valid because we're all using that same power.

ROBERT H

THINGS I FIND CHALLENGING

Living is a challenge, making it through the day. At college, a teacher says, 'I want this essay done by Tuesday.' You think, 'I'm not going to be able to get it done.' Or someone tests what you believe in. Or you hear someone make a statement and think, 'No, no, that's not right. Hang on a minute ...' Then it's certainly a challenge to go up to that person and say something.

When I was about fifteen or sixteen, a group of us were in the library at my secondary school. Some lads had got a book out and were looking at a photograph in it of a black girl and a white boy sitting together on the same bench. One of the lads made a comment like, 'What are they doing sitting together? They shouldn't be sitting together.' I could just about bite my tongue at that. But when another said, 'She should be glad she's got the right to sit on that bench with a white man', I leapt up and laid into them: 'That's such an unbelievable statement. Everyone's got a right to be who they are. They've got the same right as anyone else. How can you say that?'

I felt that, yes, maybe I'd got through to them slightly, but I certainly felt that they'd probably go away and say the same thing again. One outburst wasn't going to change the world, especially when these attitudes were shared by other people. The number of black people and people from ethnic minorities in our school would have been less than five out of about a thousand.

But I'm glad I did it. People say, 'You're a pacifist. You must sit on the fence all the time.' But being a pacifist doesn't mean you have to be passive. Often you have to be more active, to stop aggression or aggressive attitudes in the first place. You have to try and show people that there's a better way of solving problems than going off and hitting people or insulting them.

COLLETTE W

43

L etting go of my thinking-power is what I find challenging. I was in a group studying with some very wise people – not Quakers, as it happened – and one affectionately but quite pointedly described me as a 'head-case'. I think that's very accurate. At school, my life was very much centred around hard academic work, the subjects that needed the most thinking-power, like mathematics, science, physics. I've carried that on into the rest of my life. I've aspired to being an intellectual. It's been my defence against the world.

Now as I enter what I suppose is the second part of my life, I feel it's more important to let go of that, to let other sides of me come out – the feeling side, the discerning side, above all. Sometimes, when I'm in the company of wise people, I can let go. But I'm also very good at finding obstacles when I'm on my own.

Then there's the challenge not to withdraw from things. When I come across homeless people asking for money in the street, when I read about massacres in the news, the temptation is to switch off, to protect myself from hurt by backing off. That's something that intellectuals are very good at doing. If we see a problem we go away and write a paper about it. I know that's a temptation for me. The challenge is to stay involved.

PERRY

W hen I'm set a task, I tend to look at it and think, 'That's a little bit more than I can cope with.' Within the last eighteen months, after thirty-odd years of trying, I've finally managed to swim. The challenge wasn't so much the learning how as believing I would ever be a swimmer. When I realized I could be a swimmer, instead of thinking I'd never be one, it was a breakthrough. The challenge was believing I could do it.

PAULINE W

44

I 'm fairly shy, and I find that challenging. Working with other people can be difficult. But part of my job is to teach and to talk to other people – otherwise no-one would know what kind of research I'm doing!

PETER

L iving up to my ideals is very challenging. My father showed his practical commitment to peace first as a conscientious objector then working for peace on the Quaker peace committee. I find it difficult to stand in the market-place on a peace witness. I feel very humble when I think what little I have done to help relieve the huge distress of the world in a social way. Peace isn't just the absence of war, it's removing the causes of war, like human aggression. But I remember when I last witnessed for peace thinking, 'Who am I to ask other people how they lead their lives?' I find that very difficult to do. I have done it occasionally, but not very often.

I went on a CND march when I was younger and I can think of four times when I've stood silently with a group with placards in the middle of town on a Saturday. I do feel strongly that the arms trade is responsible for a lot of the trouble in the world. If people sell armaments, if armaments are readily available, then there will be destruction. I feel I should be doing more in Friends Against the Armaments Trade.

Challenges are not all uncomfortable. Trying to be a faithful Friend is challenging and has brought richness and joy into my life.

DAPHNE

FACT-FINDER

Conscientious objector
Someone who refuses to join the armed forces on conscience grounds.

Peace witness
Public demonstration of commitment to peace.

CND
Campaign for Nuclear Disarmament.

Friend(s)
Member(s) of the Society of Friends, i.e. Quaker(s).

I feel I'm not really a very good Quaker because there is quite a high standard. You have to do a lot of it from within yourself. There's no rule book to go by, no creed, no religious ceremonies to be performed – but the *Book of Discipline* helps!

I find it difficult to pray regularly, to think and meditate regularly. I'm much more of a busy person than I should be. I tend to rush around. It might be reasonably useful stuff I'm doing, but I find it difficult actually to stop and sit and just be and pray. Spirituality does not come easily to me. I'm more of a doler-out of soup!

ROSMARIE H

FACT-FINDER

Creed
Formal statement of religious belief, like those recited in some church services.

Book of Discipline
See page 20.

I find the very good suggestion that Quakers should make a silent space for prayer every day very challenging. I managed to do it for a year when I was living in America because I didn't have many friends out there. But over here I have my research and my university teaching responsibilities and lots of friends. Now I'm not so good at keeping that silent space for prayer, and I miss it.

I also find the requirement to live honestly and simply very challenging because it's so easy to dodge. Living honestly is more than not telling lies. It's being honest in my dealings with other people, being open to other people, not putting on a front. Living simply is being able to say no to things you want to buy and things you want to do so you can keep your priorities clear. It's good to be able to make space in your life so that you can focus on the one or two things that really matter to you. Having lots of possessions and taking on lots of commitments can start cluttering it up.

The thing I still feel bad about, the challenge I still haven't risen to, is inequality of wealth. I'm comfortably off. I have a nice house and nice possessions. It's never been a bother for me to afford to do anything. Several times, I've felt I ought to try to do more, give up more.

For several years I was on the national committee Quaker Social Responsibility and Education. We had residential weekends with talks and discussions on different themes, one of which was poverty and inequality. I remember how that really threw me. I came away thinking, 'I've got a good salary. My husband's got a good salary. We don't really need them both.' I seriously considered giving up my job or giving away half of what I earned.

As a family, we've always given a very high proportion of our income to charities and to Quaker work. When we first came to Cambridge, we had several years when we didn't have a car. A few years ago, we moved into a smaller house because we didn't think it was right to have a big house with empty rooms in it when so many people are homeless. We still seem to be very comfortable, though, and I find this extremely challenging.

JANET G

What I find challenging is living up to what, if I were pressed, I would have to describe as my ideals. It's a challenge I conspicuously fail to meet.

I'm very aware that I put off to tomorrow things that could be done and ways of living that could be put into practice today. I don't think I've forgotten them, but I'm often dissatisfied with myself and intending to do better. I do find it a frequent challenge that the will isn't as active as it should be.

COLIN G

INDEX

Page numbers in **bold** type show where words or phrases are explained in FACT-FINDERS